Lone Ranger Mentality
ALONE!

Unmasking the Truth About the Sin of Self-Sufficiency

BRENDA A. JENKINS

*Priority*ONE
publications
Detroit, MI USA

Leaving the Lone Ranger Mentality – Alone!
Copyright © 2003 Brenda A. Jenkins.

Reprinted from HELP! for Your Leadership, Chapter 3.
Used by Permission

All scripture quotations, unless otherwise indicated, are taken from the HOLY BIBLE, NEW INTERNATIONAL VERSION®. NIV®. Copyright ©1973, 1978, 1984 by International Bible Society. Used by permission of Zondervan. All rights reserved.

Scripture quotations marked (AMP) are taken from the Amplified Bible, Copyright © 1954, 1958, 1962, 1964, 1965, 1987 by The Lockman Foundation. Used by permission.

Out of reverence and honor for God's Word, the word Bible is capitalized throughout this work. Also throughout this work the name of satan is not capitalized in order to re-emphasize Christ's victory over him.

All rights reserved. No part of this publication may be reproduced, stored in a retrieval system, or transmitted in any form or by any means – electronic, mechanical, photocopy, recording, or any other – except for brief quotations in printed reviews, without the prior permission of the publisher.

*Priority*ONE Publications
P. O. Box 725 • Farmington, MI 48332
(800) 331-8841 Nationwide Toll Free
(313) 893-3359 Southeast Michigan
E-mail: info@p1pubs.com
URL: http://www.p1pubs.com

ISBN: 0-9703634-3-5

Cover and interior design by PriorityONE Publications
Printed in the United States of America

Table of Contents

1. Introduction 1
2. Current Condition 3
3. God's Directive 6
4. A Path to Fellowship 9
5. Possible Barriers to Fellowship 12
6. Two Biblical Characters 18
7. Scenarios 19

References 29

About Brenda A. Jenkins 31

Introduction

People grow through experience if they meet life honestly and courageously.
- Eleanor Roosevelt

I have heard people say, "I do not need people, as long I have God, I am OK." Others may feel they are self-sufficient within themselves and in need of no one. The latter is what has been called the Lone Ranger Mentality. Neither perspective is in line with God's purpose for His creation.

When you come into difficult relationships in your daily life, do you examine yourself? Does what you are doing match God's standards of relating to His people? Being obedient to God's Word leads to fellowship with Him and others. We are all a part of a bigger purpose. God wants all of us to work together using our skills and gifts.

Being a Lone Ranger disconnects you from God's purpose for you, and it disconnects you from others. There is your way, the other person's way, and God's way. Does your way match God's way? Does it glorify Him?

"As a prisoner for the Lord, then, I urge you to live a life worthy of the calling you have received. Be completely humble and gentle; be patient, bearing with one another in love. Make every effort to keep the unity of the Spirit through the bond of peace. There is one body and one Spirit--just as you were called to one hope when you were called-- one Lord, one faith, one baptism; one God and Father of all, who is over all and through all and in all. But to each one of us grace has been given as Christ apportioned it" (Ephesians 4: 1-7).

It is because of grace and mercy that God accepts us. God loves us just as we are. Ask yourself, "Am I showing grace and mercy to all people?" When confusion appears, know that confusion is not of God. Because of Jesus Christ you are victorious over satan.

When we begin to look at people as God does, we may see them differently. When we love God with all our being, we will obey Him. Through obedience to God, Who is love, we will love each other.

This chapter will be devoted to fellowship, both vertical and horizontal. I will discuss God's original design of man and how our fellowship, both with God and others will bring us to a more fruitful fulfillment in life. I will look at trust, individual responsibility, crossing our boundaries, accountability, plus sharing of self, forgiveness, and reconciliation.

If you are willing to put off sinful ways, renew your mind, and put on righteousness, (Ephesians 4:22–24) you will be able to have the more fulfilled life that God intended for you to have. Be honest with yourself and know that it is a continuous process that we will experience as long as we are in the flesh.

Also included will be two Biblical examples about forgiveness and reconciliation. I will discuss possible scenarios a person may have in their relationships with others and provide some suggestions for targeted areas for change.

Current Condition

In the introduction of Dr. Tony Evans' book, *The Kingdom Agenda*, he discusses a world off target. A world where there is chaos starting from individuals extending to the world problems we are facing today. He states, "The refusal of people to take personal responsibility for their actions has become a national epidemic. Everyone is playing the blame game" (Evans, 1999, p. 56). Take a good look at yourself and ask these questions: "Who am I? What is my purpose? Do I take responsibility for the areas in which I am responsible?"

With all the technological advancements, spending time with your neighbor has been limited. We have attached garages, working people rarely see their neighbors. Many homes have decks on the back of their homes with bushes or trees for privacy and many homes are built without front porches. When you call a company, you get a voice mail not a human being to talk with. Many take care of banking business through electronic funds transfer or Automated Teller Machine (ATM). Even at the gas station you can get gas without talking with a human being. With all the time management theories and gadgets, we have learned to occupy most of our time. Where and when is the fellowship taking place? Some of us even schedule time with God.

I read Dr. Michael A. Proud, Jr.'s sermon from June 30, 2002. on *Worship: A Picture with God, part 2*. Dr. Proud discussed how freedom is a double-edged sword that must be kept in check or it will destroy believers. He states,

"Living in a free society as we do, that concept of freedom and independence can evade every part of our lives, even our spiritual lives. It can create in our minds a lone-ranger mentality of life, that is, I don't need anyone and I can live as I like" (Proud, 2002, para 8).

As we grow closer to God and depend on Him, doing things our way is not an option. To do things our way puts us out of fellowship with God and one another. Dr. Proud states, "Yet, our love affair with independence can hinder our willingness to depend upon God and on others" (Proud, 2002, para 8).

What a lonely life this can be. God made us to be relational beings. He created Adam for Himself and then He created Eve for Adam.

In the very beginning, it was to be that vertical relationship with God and that horizontal relationship with Eve. He commanded Adam and Eve to populate the earth. That was their purpose. So together as man and wife, they began populating the earth (Genesis). Man was created in God's own image. Woman was created as a helpmate for man. All of humanity comes from Adam and Eve. Our relationship is with God and each other.

God's Directive

All through scripture we are told to love one another. If you love God, you will love others (I John 4:7-8).

If anyone says, "I Love God," yet hates his brother, he is a liar. For anyone who does not love his brother, whom he has seen, can not love God, whom he has not seen. I John 4:20

The Daily Walk Bible Calendar, on the December 18, 1993 states,

"Fellowship is a shared conviction, a shared commitment, a shared compassion. It is two people walking the same road, bearing the same load. Fellowship involves a vertical dimension with the Father and a horizontal dimension with fellow Christians."

That which was from the beginning, which we have heard, which we have seen with our eyes, which we have looked at and our hands have touched — this we proclaim concerning the Word of life. The life appeared; we have seen it and testify to it, and we proclaim to you the eternal life, which was with the Father and has appeared to us. We proclaim to you what we have seen and heard, so that you also may have fellowship with us. And our fellowship is with the Father and with his Son, Jesus Christ. We write this to make our joy complete. This is the message we have heard from him and declare to you: God is light; in him there is no darkness at all. 1 John 1:1-5

All of us belong to God. Only God knows each of us totally. True love puts an end to anger, resentment, and bitterness. We must replace our reactions to people with God's reaction.

This is truly a testing time for us Christians. Because of the pain many of us have endured in our lives, the sinful nature attempts to protect us from those who created pain for us, and those who are different from us. The test comes when we don't agree. It's very easy to practice love with those who have the same values as we do.

Think about the "s" word (submission). True submission is when you disagree but submit to the person in authority based on God's Word.

Do many of us become solo to prevent ourselves from submitting? Do you become solo so you don't have to love? How many people (and this could be those in leadership) want things done their way?

My question would be, "Is your way God's way?" The love affair you are commanded to have with God requires you to die to self, love your enemies, and pray for those who curse you.

Loving one another in this sinful world hurts. Remember the cost that our Lord paid for His relationship with us.

A new commandment I give to you: Love one another. As I have loved you, so you must love one another. By this all men will know you are my disciples, if you love one another. John 13: 34-35

If you obey my commands, you will remain in my love, just as I have obeyed my Father's commands and remain in his love. I have told you this so that my joy may be in you and that your joy may be complete. My command is this: Love each other as I have loved you. John 15: 10–12

Jesus calls us His friends because of the knowledge He passed on to us in His word. Everything He learned from His Father is passed on to us (John 15:15). Do we share what we learn with others (family, co-workers, ministry team workers, friends, etc.)?

A Path to Fellowship

I would like to share a path you can use to develop fellowship with God and man by obeying Jesus' greatest commandments *(Matthew 22:37, 39).*

I. Love the Lord your God with all your heart, and with all your soul and with all your strength and with all of your mind.

Psalm 63 KJV does an excellent job of explaining our fellowship with God.

God's presence

1 O God, thou art my God; early will I seek thee: my soul thirsteth for thee, my flesh longeth for thee in a dry and thirsty land, where no water is;

2 To see thy power and thy glory, so as I have seen thee in the sanctuary.

God's love

3 Because thy lovingkindness is better than life, my lips shall praise thee.

4 Thus will I bless thee while I live: I will lift up my hands in thy name.

5 My soul shall be satisfied as with marrow and fatness; and my mouth shall praise thee with joyful lips:

God's knowledge of you

6 When I remember thee upon my bed, and meditate on thee in the night watches.

7 Because thou hast been my help, therefore in the shadow of thy wings will I rejoice.

8 My soul followeth hard after thee: thy right hand upholdeth me.

9 But those that seek my soul, to destroy it, shall go into the lower parts of the earth.

10 They shall fall by the sword: they shall be a portion for foxes.

11 But the king shall rejoice in God; every one that sweareth by him shall glory: but the mouth of them that speak lies shall be stopped.

Another scripture showing God's love is Psalm 103:11, 17, which gives the heights and depth of God's love toward us. You must look at Psalm 139:1–10, God knows and accepts us. He is with us through our every situation. He is everywhere. Fellowship with God is the foundation of your fellowship with man, so likewise…

II. Love your neighbor as yourself.

You ask the question, "How do I love my neighbor? I know the Scripture, but how do I do that? I can't stand the pain."

I am glad you asked the question. You cannot do it by yourself. It is vital that you get the knowledge of God's Word and pray for wisdom to apply the Word in your everyday life. You can't do it by yourself. It is crucial that you understand redemption. You ask, "How do I get started?" The answer is to first seek the kingdom of heaven (Matthew 6:33). Your mind is to be on God's desires, heavenly things (Phil. 4: 8).

In John 14:6, Jesus said, "I am the way, the truth, and the life." Our most important relationship is the relationship we have with

God through His son Jesus Christ. Our makeup is unique – no human can completely satisfy us.

As we grow in the Lord, we must do more than share what God has done for us. We must direct people to God's Word.

As Christians, we have God's grace. We must remember the sacrifice (Jesus) that permitted us to be united back with our Creator in perfect union. It is through grace and mercy that we are saved. Let Jesus be Lord of your life. He provides peace and joy in our lives.

Possible Barriers to Fellowship

In the name of Jesus, we have power to overcome sin. Why are we allowing sin to continue to separate us from God and our fellow man? We were born in sin, but Jesus paid the price for us. We must accept Jesus as our Lord and Savior. We must die to self.

Do you know what your responsibilities are, and what God's responsibilities are? Doing the responsibilities of others can create a barrier in the relationship. The following chart may assist you in determining your responsibilities. Remember Jesus saves. The Holy Spirit clears my mind so that I won't get confused, unless I am trying to figure out something that I need to leave in God's capable hands.

Listed below are some responsibilities of the 5 R's sorted by God versus Man.

Chart #1 – 5 R's - © 2000 Brenda A. Jenkins

(GOD) Father, Son, and the Holy Spirit	Man
Responsibility Creator & Finisher (Alpha & Omega) Gives Grace Provides Promises	**Responsibility** Make your bodies living sacrifice Rom. 12:1 Make Jesus Lord of your life, be obedient to God's Word
Redemption God sent His only begotten son, Jesus Christ to pay the price for our sins He died on the Cross, rose, and sits on the right hand of God. God's <u>Word</u> gives the Revelation of Redemption	Redemption We must be in agreement with God's verdict on sin in the cross of Jesus Christ We must have a conscious experience of salvation in our lives

Reconciliation Reconciliation between God and Man God brings us back to Himself by blotting out our sins and making us righteous He reestablished relationship (God & Man)	**Reconciliation** Ministry of reconciliation II Cor 5:18-19 Reconciliation between Man and Man Matt 5: 23-24 KJV Therefore if thou bring thy gift to the altar, and there rememberest that thy brother hath aught against thee: Leave there thy gift before the altar, and go thy way; first be reconciled to thy brother, and then come and offer thy gift Our relationship with each other affects our relationship with God.
Regeneration Jesus sent the Holy Spirit to be with us until his return (strength)	**Regeneration** Let the Holy Spirit control your life.
Restoration Second coming, New earth, Bible begins with the majestic story of creation of the universe and it concludes with the creation of a new Heaven and earth Rev. 21:1-5	**Restoration** Knowledge of God's Word Rom 15:14 and Col 3:16 Know the word and how to apply it Gal 6:1 Restore others, Remember, Love one another, Glorify God, First teach yourself, then teach others

Another barrier that may interfere with relationships with one another is trust. What makes a person appear to not be trustworthy? Are you a trustworthy person? Trust can break down if someone:

- Is a backstabber
- Exploits you
- Consistently breaks promises
- Misleads you in some way
- Gossips about you
- Rejects you
- Breaks an agreement or contract
- Withholds important information from you
- Takes credit for your work
- Criticizes you unfairly

We all know that the only person we can change is ourselves. We are uniquely made. It is possible for someone to have a different interpretation of words and actions based on their make-up (physical, mental, and moral). God's Word is the same yesterday, today, and tomorrow. Perfection is only in God. We are connected through Jesus Christ. God's Word will help lead us when it comes to dealing with others. The following chart has some possible instructions for dealing with trust issues both within you and with others.

"Trust is the highest form of human motivation. It brings out the very best in people."
Stephen R. Covey,
The 7 Habits of Highly Effective People

Chart #2
Truth Scriptures Based On Yours and Other's Actions
© 2003 Brenda A. Jenkins

Your Actions	Possible Impact on others	God's Word	Other's Actions	What God's Word tells you to do
Backstab others	May feel like they have been stabbed	Eph. 4:25 Proverbs 11:3 Proverbs 12:17 Proverbs 25:18	Backstab you	Hebrews 12:2-3 Proverbs 12:6, 13
Exploit others	Person may feel used	Proverbs 16:11 Proverbs 20:10	Exploit you	Proverbs 15:3
Consistently breaks promises	May feel let down	Genesis 4:7	Fails to keep promises	Proverbs 12:22
Mislead someone	May feel they can't depend on the person	Proverbs 14:25 Eph. 4:29	Misleads you in some way	James 1:19
Gossip about others	May feel excluded	Proverbs 13:3	Gossip about you	1 Peter 5:8-9 James 3:8

Your Actions	Possible Impact on others	God's Word	Other's Actions	What God's Word tells you to do
Reject someone	Person may feel unwanted	1 Peter 3:10-11 Romans 16:17	Rejects you	Proverbs 12:16 Proverbs 19:11
Break agreement or contract	Person may feel disappointed	Genesis 3:15 Genesis 15:12-21, 17:1-14 Hebrews 8:6-13	Breaks an agreement or contract	Proverbs 22:20
Do not provide important information	May feel setup to look bad, or to fail	John 15:15	Withholds important information from you	Proverbs 8:23-24
Takes credit for someone else's work	May feel betrayed	Proverbs 21:3	Takes credit for your work	Philippians 4:13
Criticizes someone else unfairly	Closeness may be broken when judging and criticism begin	John 8:7	Criticizes you unfairly	James 2:13 Proverbs 9:7-9

God's Word supplies many Scriptures. These are ones that helped me. You may have to search for others to help you. Let the Holy Spirit lead you. Meditate on Psalm 37.

This is a time for us to be humble. We know we are nothing. We must thank the Father for living within us. This is a time of healing. Let God love you and pamper you; He is truly the only One that can totally satisfy and understand you. Thank Him for He is truly worthy. Spending time with God is a prerequisite for anything you do.

Relationships with one another are what Jesus commanded us to do in Love. If you miss that fellowship, you don't operate efficiently (to full capacity).

Two biblical characters from the Bible being advised by Paul to be reconciled

☐. **In Philemon verses 8-28**

Paul appeals to Philemon to forgive his runaway slave, Onesimus, and to accept him as a brother in the faith. He asked him not to punish him, but to forgive and restore him as a new Christian brother.

Christian relationships must be full of forgiveness and acceptance. Can you forgive those who have wronged you? We need to get pass barriers that work to separate us and be courteous and respectful, loving one another as God loves us.

2. **Philippians ☐:2-3 Reconciliation**

At the church, two women were having relationship problems. They had been working for years for Christ in the Church. Their broken relationship was no small matter.

Because many had become believers through their efforts, there was no excuse for remaining un-reconciled. Paul encouraged them to become reconciled.

Are you in a broken relationship? Look in God's Word. It is specific on how we are to reconcile with others. Remember, all have sinned. Treat others as God has treated you. You may say they don't deserve your forgiveness, or they sinned against you. Get in the presence of God. Now, ask yourselves, do you deserve His forgiveness and have you sinned?

Scenarios

Scenario ☐: What if you are a loner and you do not have someone you can be intimate with? You associate with people, but there is no one to help when you are down. You may or may not have an intimate relationship with God.

Suggestions:

First, it is important that you know the difference between being alone and being lonely. Being alone involves physical separation from others. Many times this is what we desire. It could be for rest, to get our thoughts together, communicating with God, or just a time to be alone.

Being lonely includes both spiritual and psychological isolation. If the situation is that you are truly lonely, you have two choices. The lonely person can rise above the loneliness, or stay in it, suffering the consequences. We were not created to be alone.

As you read the pages of this chapter, I pray you realize it is because of you that these words are being written. You are more than a conqueror with Jesus. The intent is to help leaders recognize they are not alone. Being alone is a choice. Meditate on the following scriptures.

John 15:15 – Jesus is your friend.
Hebrew 13:5 – God assures us He will never let us down.
Hebrew 12:2 – Stay focused on Jesus, our Guide and Savior.

Another resource is *Lonely But Never Alone* by J. Oswald Sanders.

Scenario 2:

Those very close to you are in pain because of sin in their lives. Because of your love for them, you also feel pain. You may be able on some level to relate to the pain they are going through. You see their mistakes. You feel helpless because you can't help them. You don't want to fall with your loved one, as you have done in the past. Being an overachiever (survivor) you know how to get back up when you fall. You get back in the race. You are broken once more.

The question is, "What do you do?" Do you get as far away from them as possible? What if it this is your spouse, parent, child, brother, or sister?

Suggestions:

Pray and ask God for guidance. Know yourself. Know your boundaries. Know what you are responsible for. This is a good time to write out what your role is with this person. Have you crossed boundaries and taken on their responsibilities? Have you detached yourself from this person? Detachment is not separation. Many times in close relationships we lose ourselves.

Ask yourself what would Jesus do? Do not throw the relationship away. God did not throw us away. Love is the most potent weapon in this universe. Love the person as God has loved you. This is a time for intercessory prayer. In Hebrews 4:15 Jesus interceded for us as our High Priest.

In Galatians 6:1b, we are warned to be careful lest we fall. You can tell the person you love them, and God loves them more. If this is an unsaved person, this is your opportunity to tell them about Jesus. Tell them what Jesus has done for you. Tell them how they can also be saved. Christians should apply reconciliation Scriptures.

Salvation scriptures to share:

Many study Bibles have salvation scriptures that you can use for yourself and share with others. To be effective in sharing with someone, it is important that you believe the Scriptures in your heart and show others by your example. To read them in the following order makes an awesome impact.

John 3:16	John 10:10
Romans 3:23	Romans 5:8
I Corinthians 15:3-6	John 14:5
John 1:12	Ephesians 2:8, 9
John 3:1-8	Revelations 3:20

Christian to Christian:

If they are in right standing, confessing their sins, asking for forgiveness, and working on living in righteousness (I John 1:9), use reconciliation Scriptures such as Matthew 5:23-24.

> *Therefore if thou bring thy gift to the altar, and there rememberest that thy brother hath aught against thee; Leave there thy gift before the altar, and go thy way; first be reconciled to thy brother, and then come and offer thy gift.*

Scenario 3: Dealing with someone who criticizes you. The person does not take responsibility for anything that happens. From your frame of reference, they are taking on the role of a victim. When you are around the person, the two of you clash. You are very different. The two of you create pain for each other.

Suggestions:

Recognize that this person may have internal issues with relationships. You have to ask yourself, "Why am I reacting to this person?" If you are feeling pain, there may be some unresolved issues within yourself. People, who are hurting, hurt other people.

Talk with God about your feelings. Ask for help, healing whatever is within you that makes you react. Pain is a sign that something needs to be changed. As far as the other person is concerned, love them like God told you to love them. You may need to work on developing a relationship with this person.

Ask yourself, "What do I know about this person? Do I trust the person?"

You may want to do the self-assessment on trust. Make changes as the Word instructs you to. The situation you have may be two people with issues. You are responsible for yours. As the Scripture says in Ephesians 4:22-24, do put on and put off those things you are responsible for.

Also, you must become an intercessory prayer warrior for the other person. The Bible said reconciliation is our ministry (Matthew 5: 23-24). Trust God that all things will work together for those who love Him (Romans 8: 28). Always look at what improvements can be done in your life. Be at peace with all men.

Summary

I would like to share an experience I had at a meeting in my home with a couple of my girlfriends. I am always trying to get as much done as possible on the days I have at home.

This particular Saturday morning I decided to have the refrigerator repairman repair the icemaker, and the washing machine and dryer repairman come out and repair these two appliances. After all, I was going to be at home.

I scheduled two meetings at my home that day: my writer's group (girlfriends) meeting and my family reunion committee meeting later that day.

The repairman for the washing machine and dryer came at 9:00 a.m. Hallelujah! He was done before my 10:00 a.m. meeting with my girlfriends.

The repairman for the refrigerator came in the middle of our meeting. It was OK because we were in the dining room. The dining room is adjacent to the kitchen. Any information he needed from me, I could give him and still continue with my meeting.

When he completed the repair of the refrigerator, I had to go over to the refrigerator so he could explain what he fixed. When I looked behind the refrigerator and saw all the mess behind it, there was no way I could let him return the refrigerator to its original place without doing some major clean up. I had to do more than just sweep. It needed some personal cleaning up to get down to the root.

I told the repairman to leave the refrigerator where it was and I would move it back after I cleaned the area behind the refrigerator. He left, and I returned to my meeting.

My girlfriend said, "I know you are going to write about that?" My response was, "What do you mean?" She said, "After you saw the mess behind the refrigerator; you said it must be cleaned. Think about that when it comes to God showing us things."

My question, readers, for you to ponder is, "Has there been some mess identified in your life that needs to be cleaned up before you can move back to your original place with God, or are you going to cover it up, deep within your heart, thinking it won't affect anything? Won't it start smelling after a while and affect other things?"

We all need the loving connection of God. Living in this world we are going to experience pain. Being connected to God through Jesus with the help of the Holy Spirit is what protects us when we experience pain. Being obedient means to deny self and depend totally on Him. God is love and we must give love to one another. In this way, we will receive love. Remember to ask God for help (James 4:6). God I need help. Know what you are responsible for and turn those other things over to God. You can't save anyone. Jesus saves (1 Peter 5:7 cast your worries on Him). Take one day at a time. Do not worry about tomorrow (Matthew 6:34).

"He must turn from evil and do good; he must seek peace and pursue it" (1 Peter 3:11).

Heavenly Father, I praise You and thank You for loving me. I thank You for Your Son Who died on the cross for my transgressions. I thank You for the Holy Spirit that dwells within me. Continue Your work in me, for Lord I know I am a work in process. Help me to stay focused on You and to do Your will in all areas of my life. Help me to be obedient to Your Word and be in fellowship with You and my fellow man. In the Name of Jesus – Amen.

References

1 Cloud, H. and Townsend, J. *Safe People* (1995). Zondervan, Grand Rapids, MI

2 Evans, Tony. *The Kingdom Agenda: What A Way to Live.* (1999). Word Publishing; Nashville, TN

3 Jenkins, Brenda A. *Accepting Your Spiritual Heritage* (November 18, 2000). Workshop Presentation at Midwest Biblical Counseling Conference. Detroit, MI

4 Proud, Michael A. *Worship: A Picture of Intimacy with God pt.2* (Retrieved April 28, 2003), URL:http://www.thetrinitytouch.com/sermons/6-30-02.html.

5 Sanders, Oswald J. *Lonely But Never Alone*. Grand Rapids, MI. Radio Bible Class

6 *The Daily Walk Calendar.* (December 18, 1993). Wheaton, IL. Tyndale Calendars

About Brenda A. Jenkins

Brenda loves people. She states her purpose is to take her gifts and skills to help others. She is very transparent and has no problem sharing her victories overcoming rough times in her life. Brenda has the ability to see the expected outcome of any task and works to put plans in place to reach that end.

Brenda is well-versed in problem-solving, organizational and interpersonal skills. The Foundation for all that she does rests in her strong commitment to the Word of God. She is the mother to four adult children and the proud grandmother to twelve grandchildren.

At New Hope Missionary Baptist Church in Southfield, Michigan, Brenda served faithfully for seven years as the Ministry Director of the Biblical Counseling Ministry; a ministry birthed under her leadership. Currently, she is the Counseling Advisor and Outreach Facilitator for this ministry. As a Certified Biblical Counselor and adjunct instructor for Christian Research and Development, she teaches classes that will build up students and prepare them to confront themselves and counsel others with the Bible as the guidebook.

As CEO of ARIEL Connections her passion is "Providing Relationship Solutions to Organizations that Value People."

For more information or to book Ms. Jenkins for speaking engagements, or radio and television interviews contact:

ARIEL Connections
P.O. Box 22, Royal Oak, MI 48068-0022
email: brenda.jenkins@ameritech.net
website: ariel-connections.com
Phone: (313) 719-1621

A - Accept
R - Relate
I - Invest
E - Encourage
L - Love

When We Reach the Edge, Where Do We Go for Support?

Name _____
Address _____
City _____ State _____ Zip_____
Phone _____ Fax _____
Email _____

Quantity	
Price *(each)*	$4.99
Subtotal	
S & H *(each)*	$0.99
MI Tax 6%	
TOTAL	

When We Reach the Edge, Where Do We Go For Support?
BRENDA A. JENKINS

METHOD OF PAYMENT:
❏ Check or Money Order
(*Make payable to*: **PriorityONE Publications**)
❏ Visa ❏ Master Card ❏ American Express
Acct No. _____
Expiration Date (*mmyy*) _____
Signature _____

Mail your payment with this form to:
PriorityONE Publications
P. O. Box 725, Farmington, MI 48332
(800) 331-8841 – Toll Free
(313) 893-3359 – Southeast Michigan
URL: http://www.p1pubs.com
Email: info@p1pubs.com

Leaving the
Lone Ranger Mentality – Alone!

Name _____
Address _____
City _____ State _____ Zip _____
Phone _____ Fax _____
Email _____

Quantity	
Price *(each)*	$4.99
Subtotal	
S & H *(each)*	$0.99
MI Tax 6%	
TOTAL	

METHOD OF PAYMENT:
❏ Check or Money Order
(*Make payable to*: **PriorityONE Publications**)
❏ Visa ❏ Master Card ❏ American Express
Acct No. _____
Expiration Date (*mmyy*) _____
Signature _____

Mail your payment with this form to:
PriorityONE Publications
P. O. Box 725, Farmington, MI 48332
(800) 331-8841 – Toll Free
(313) 893-3359 – Southeast Michigan
URL: http://www.p1pubs.com
Email: info@p1pubs.com

HELP! for Your Leadership

Name _____
Address _____
City _____ State _____ Zip_____
Phone _____ Fax _____
Email _____

Quantity	
Price *(each)*	$14.99
Subtotal	
S & H *(each)*	$2.99
MI Tax 6%	
TOTAL	

METHOD OF PAYMENT:
❑ Check or Money Order
(*Make payable to*: **PriorityONE Publications**)
❑ Visa   ❑ Master Card   ❑ American Express
Acct No. _____
Expiration Date (*mmyy*) _____
Signature _____

Mail your payment with this form to:
PriorityONE Publications
P. O. Box 725, Farmington, MI 48332
(800) 331-8841 – Toll Free
(313) 893-3359 – Southeast Michigan
URL: http://www.p1pubs.com
Email: info@p1pubs.com

Be on the lookout for these future books by
Brenda A. Jenkins

(2005). Black, Sabrina D., Dixon, Christina, Hudson, Pamela J., and Jenkins, Brenda A. *HELP! for Your Leadership Leaders Self Care Workbook*. Detroit, Michigan; PriorityONE Publications

(2005). *ARIEL Connections Relationship Model: Building Relationships that Last*. Detroit, Michigan; PriorityONE Publications

(2006). *"Out of Your Pain: "You Are Who You Are"*. (TNT) Detroit, Michigan; PriorityONE Publications

(2006). *"HELP! for Parents"*. (TNT) Detroit, Michigan; PriorityONE Publications